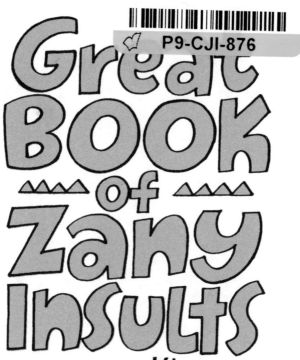

Great Book of Zany Insults

by Gene Perret

ILLUSTRATED by Sanford Hoffman

Sterling Publishing Co., Inc.
New York

[Great Book of Zany Insults]

10 9 8 7 6 5 4 3 2 1

Published 1996 by Sterling Publishing Company, Inc.
387 Park Avenue South, New York, N.Y. 10016
Originally published under the title *Funny Comebacks
to Rude Remarks* © 1990 by Gene Perret
Distributed in Canada by Sterling Publishing
c/o Canadian Manda Group, One Atlantic Avenue, Suite 105
Toronto, Ontario, Canada M6K 3E7
Distributed in Great Britain and Europe by Cassell PLC
Wellington House, 125 Strand, London WC2R 0BB, England
Distributed in Australia by Capricorn Link (Australia) Pty Ltd.
P.O. Box 6651, Baulkham Hills, Business Centre, NSW 2153, Australia
Manufactured in the United States of America

Sterling ISBN 0-8069-9408-8

To
Michael and Brett Maurer
May they always have laughter

Contents

AUTHOR'S NOTE TO THE READER:

Insult humor today has become a sign of good fellowship. When friends get together they enjoy taunting one another with clever put-downs.

Like puppies in a playful fight, they snarl, growl, and snap at one another, but they don't really do any harm. They don't inflict any wounds.

This is a collection of snappy wisecracks that I used to exchange with my buddies when I was a kid. There are also some comebacks that I've written. I wish I had thought of them back then, but I didn't.

They're here now for you. I hope you'll enjoy them and use them in a friendly way. Laughter is a joyous, happy thing. Humor loses much of its charm when it's used to attack, to hurt.

Will Rogers was one of America's most beloved comedians in the 1920's and 30's. He kidded most of the famous people of his time, but they weren't hurt by his wisecracks. Will Rogers explained it by saying, "If there's no malice in your heart, there can't be none in your jokes."

Enjoy these jokes in the spirit in which they're offered—a spirit of fun.

HOW TO
USE THIS BOOK

On the following pages I've listed several of the wisecracks that people used to throw at me, and then some snappy comebacks that I wish I had thrown back at them—then.

There's no way I can remember all the teasing they did (I was very "tease-able"), and there's no way I can predict what smart aleck remarks they'll toss at you.

So I've grouped the comebacks to answer one nasty insult—it's easy to see how they work that way. You'll notice, though, that you can use these lines to respond to many different wisecracks besides the one that I listed.

For example, you don't need a Tarzan insult to say, "Look, Jane, Cheetah's learned to talk." You can say it almost any time—whenever people are trying to make a monkey out of you.

Just remember the comebacks you especially key into and file them away in your mind. Memorize them, if you like. You'll find that you'll be able to use them time and time again.

Soon people will learn to think twice before they trade wisecracks with you—because they'll never catch you without a snappy comeback!

CHAPTER 1

If You Had Any Brains—!

When they were giving out brains, I remember holding the door for you. You were the one who backed in—on stilts.

You were one of the first to get a brain. You got yours before they were perfected.

But you actually did get a brain that day. The problem is you should have asked for one to go.

You got your brain very early. Apparently, the warranty has run out.

When they were giving out brains you showed up too late. All you got was a raincheck.

They ran out of brains just when you got there. So they gave you a nice wood carving instead.

You didn't get a brain that day, either. They were only giving them to people who would use them.

You got your brain very early. They were giving them out in alphabetical order and you were under "A" for "animal."

And if your brain was a train, it would all be in the caboose.

And if your brain was a chain, it would have a couple of links missing.

And if your face was a race, nobody would win.

And if your brain was in Spain, you'd get to use it just about as much as you do now.

And if your head was a bed, it would still be unmade.

And if your brain was grain, it would be the same as it is now—oatmeal.

And if your brain was a train, it would be the same as it is now—out of steam.

And if your brain was a Great Dane, it could only hold one flea at a time.

And if your brain was a plane, they'd have to foam the runway every time it landed.

I know. When do you want it back?

That's true. And you took the head it used to be kept in.

That's all I need to outsmart you.

Well, try not to be jealous.

Would you like to borrow it for a weekend to impress your friends?

If *you* had the brain of a jackass, your grades would shoot up.

You should have the brain of a jackass. It would match the rest of you.

You have everything from the jackass except the brain.

You could have the brain of a jackass, too. Your head certainly has the room for it.

You could have the brain of a jackass, too—if you can find a jackass dumb enough to swap with you.

I heard you donated your brain to science and they gave it back.

I heard you donated your brain to science and they're using it as a paperweight . . . which is more than you ever used it for.

I heard you donated your brain to science but they had to turn it down. They don't have microscopes powerful enough to see it.

I heard you donated your brain to science and they pinned it on the bulletin board with all the other cartoons.

I heard you donated your brain to science and it's sitting in a jar on a shelf doing nothing— just like when you had it.

I heard you donated your brain to science and they didn't know what it was.

You'll never get a brain disease. Germs don't grow in a vacuum.

Your brain *is* a disease.

You'll never get a brain disease, either. You'd have no place to keep it.

You've already got a brain disease— hemorrhoids.

You could always have a brain transplant. All you'd need would be a jackass with an organ donor card.

You'll never get a brain disease, either. Any germ with an ounce of intelligence wouldn't want anything to do with you.

If you ever get a brain disease, you could cure it in no time. Take a sitz bath.

You've already got a brain disease—termites.

You had a thought once, but you figured it was a headache, took two aspirins and got rid of it.

You had a thought once, but you smothered it when you sat down.

CHAPTER 2

When They Were Giving Out Looks . . .

When they were giving out looks, you thought they said "books," and said, "Give me something funny."

When they were giving out heads, you thought they said "beds," and said, "I'd like something soft."

When they were giving out brains, you thought they said "grains," and said, "Make mine oatmeal."

When they were giving out noses, you thought they said "roses," and said, "Give me a big red one."

When they were giving out heads, you thought they said "sheds," and said, "I'll take a wooden one."

When they were giving out brains, you thought they said "canes," and said, "I can get along without one, thank you."

When they were giving out noses, you thought they said "hoses," and said, "I don't mind if mine drips a little bit."

When they were giving out faces, you thought they said "cases," and said, "I'd like one made of leather."

When they were giving out heads, you thought they said "breads," and said, "I'd like mine floating in gravy."

When you go to the beauty parlor, you have to use the emergency entrance.

At least I go to the beauty parlor. You get your work done at the body and fender shop.

Look who's talking. When they work on you at the beauty parlor they have to erect scaffolding.

They say beauty is only skin deep. On you, it hasn't even gotten that far.

Look who's talking. Where do you buy your make-up—at Lourdes?

You don't even go to the beauty parlor. You just call the paramedics.

Beauty is only skin deep, but your "ugly" goes all the way to the bone.

You don't even go into the beauty parlor. You just stand outside and beg for scraps.

You don't even have a beautician. Once a week, you just visit your local witch doctor.

Look who's talking. Your Avon lady gets hazard pay.

I hung a picture of you in my basement but the rats just thought you were one of their relatives.

That's funny. I hung a picture of you in my basement and it attracted the rats.

I hung a picture of you in my basement and it killed the rats. They died laughing.

I hung a picture of you in my basement and the rats love it. They use it to play darts.

I tried to do the same thing with your picture but the ASPCA said that would be cruelty to animals.

I don't have a picture of you, and I hope to stay that lucky for the rest of my life.

If you look up "ugly" in the dictionary, there's a picture of you there.

As long as you're around, there's no reason to look up "ugly" in the dictionary.

When you learn to read, you can use the dictionary that has words instead of pictures.

I'm glad you learned to use a dictionary. You might get your vocabulary all the way up to ten words now.

That's funny, I didn't see it there. And I had to look up "ugly" when the police asked for a description of you.

They would have put your picture there—but they already used it next to "grotesque."

I'm glad you're learning words now. For a long time your trainer only used hand signals.

CHAPTER 3

What's Your I.Q.?

Is 12 your age or your I.Q.?

Look who's talking. You can't even spell I.Q.

The only way you could get a 12 I.Q. would be to take the test twice and add the scores together.

They didn't even give you an I.Q. They knew you had no place to put it.

If you had an I.Q. of 12 you'd have to grow two more fingers to be able to count it.

Look who's talking. I know potted plants with I.Q.'s higher than yours.

You just like to say I.Q. because it's the big-gest word you know how to spell.

Maybe someday you'll have an I.Q. of 12, if you ever learn to count that high.

The only I.Q. test you ever took was working your way through a maze to find the piece of cheese hidden at the end.

I don't know what your I.Q. is, but I know it starts with a decimal point.

You have a high I.Q., but for you that stands for "Idiot Quotient."

They put out a list of people in this city who are smarter than you. It's called the phone book.

Good. Maybe you can have somebody read it to you sometime.

And they had a meeting of people in this city who are dumber than you, but it was cancelled. He caught a cold.

And they have a place for all the people in this city who look like you. Maybe you've seen it. It's called "The Zoo."

You know the phone book well. It's the only book you've ever owned that didn't have pictures in it.

They also published a list of the people in this city who are dumber than you. It's not really a book; it's a pamphlet.

All the people who are smarter than you wouldn't fit in this city.

I know the phone book. It's the only book you've ever opened.

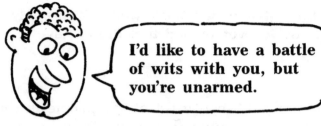

I'd like to have a battle of wits with you, but you're unarmed.

People have told me you're quite a wit. So far, it looks like they're half right.

I may be unarmed, but you're out of ammunition.

Good. Then it'll be an even fight.

With your wits I wouldn't go into battle with anyone. I'd become a peace activist.

I've heard you're a real wit—with a capital T-W-I-T.

You couldn't have a battle of wits with anyone. You've only got enough ammunition for a skirmish.

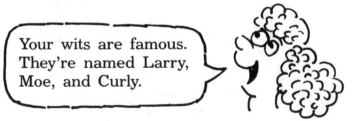

Your wits are famous. They're named Larry, Moe, and Curly.

You couldn't tell left from right if I gave you 2 guesses.

And you're the only person I know who can take a multiple choice quiz and ask for more choices.

You put both of your shoes on the same foot. It's the only way you can be sure of getting at least one right.

That's why you'll never be a paratrooper. They don't take people who can't tell "up" from "down."

You're the only person I know who can misspell her middle initial.

You look like an intelligent guy. What other impersonations do you do?

I also do a mangy dog, but you might take offense.

You look like an intelligent guy, too—but not for too long.

You look like an intelligent guy, too. But you ruin it as soon as you open your mouth.

You look like a nitwit, which is great. The toughest acting is to be yourself.

It's an easy impersonation. In the same room with you, anyone could look intelligent.

You judging intelligence is like Telly Savalas judging shampoos.

Well, I can roll over and play dead—like your brain.

CHAPTER 4

You Look Familiar. . . .

No, you probably saw me at the zoo. I was the one feeding you the peanuts.

I understand that's your favorite show because so many of your relatives are on it.

You're trying to insult me, but I know you like me. I can see your tail wagging.

That's funny. You're calling me an animal and you're the one with webbed feet.

You look familiar, too. But that's understandable. Bug collecting is my hobby.

You look familiar, too. I have a tree in my backyard. Have you ever hung from it by your tail?

Hey, Four-eyes.

What do you want, Half-head?

You're just calling me that because it's as high as you can count.

Let's not start counting body parts. You'll lose.

You should wear glasses. You'd be able to see the faces people make when you approach.

It would kill you to wear glasses. You'd look in the mirror one time and die laughing.

What is it, Six-teeth?

Some people think you're a pain in the neck. I have a much lower opinion of you.

Everything you do seems to be lower than other people.

I wouldn't want you to think badly of me. But since you rarely think at all, there's not much danger of that.

I know which part of the body you're referring to. That's where most of your opinions seem to be centered.

I didn't know you had opinions. I thought all you had was bad breath.

I value your opinions. They come in handy if I want to make a fool of myself.

When I want your opinion, I'll give it to you.

You're such a weakling, you have to get two friends to help you change your mind.

And you're such a weakling, if muscles were brains, you'd still be stupid.

And you're such a weakling, the only way you could make a muscle is with an erector set.

And you're such a weakling, you can't even hold up your end of a conversation.

And you're such a weakling, every time you throw out your chest, the trash men refuse to collect it.

And you're such a weakling, if it weren't for
your head, you'd have no muscles in your
body at all.

And you're such a weakling, the only thing
you can break with your bare hands is a
promise.

And you're such a weakling, if it weren't for
your Adam's apple, you'd have no physique
at all.

And you're such a
weakling, you can't
even lift your own
morale.

You eat like a vacuum cleaner.

I've seen you eat, too. You don't chew your food; you inhale it.

I've got a couple of ideas that should improve your table manners. They're called "a knife and a fork."

You do *everything* like a bird. A dodo bird.

You eat like a bird, too. You eat things you find on the ground.

But you really eat like a bird. They don't use a plate, either.

You eat like a bird, too. But that's all right if you like worms.

I may eat like a vulture, but you look like one.

44

I hear you donated your body to science and they had no use for it. They prefer using live monkeys.

I hear you donated your body to science and they were thrilled. They thought they had finally found the missing link.

I heard you donated your body to science and they refused to accept it. It wasn't worth the postage due.

CHAPTER 5

What a Face!

Your face would not only stop a door, but also most clocks and a charging herd of buffalo.

And if your face had "welcome" written on it, it would make a perfect doormat.

If you put your face near a door, no one would ever come in.

Your face is a mess, too. You've got to stop hammering nails with your chin.

Your face doesn't look like a doorstop. It looks like the door kept right on going.

Your face looks bad, too. Maybe you better stop reading the book before you slam it shut.

Your face looks bad, too. Maybe you should spend a few bucks and buy your dog something else to chew on.

Your face looks bad too. Maybe you should try licking the envelope *before* you drop it in the box.

Your face looks messed up, too. When you practice your swan dives from now on, you'd better make sure the pool is filled.

Your whole body's a mess. Next time you throw your clothes in the washing machine, take them off first.

Your face looks like it's been swatted across the kitchen floor a few times with a broom.

Your face looks very becoming—it's becoming more and more grotesque every minute.

And you look like dynamite—after the explosion.

And you look like the cat's meow—well, you look like some part of the cat, anyhow.

And you look like the big cheese—yessir, a real crock.

You look like a movie star—Freddie.

49

You're really dressed to kill, too. I know it's killing me.

And you're dressed to the teeth. Unfortunately, I think the outfit needs dental work.

You look like the Queen of Sheba—who, as you know, has been dead for over 2000 years.

You look like King Tut—mummified.

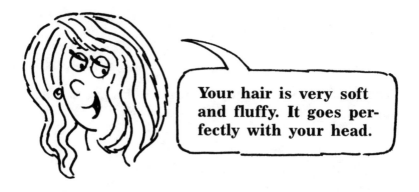

Your hair has beautiful waves in it. Of course, so do parts of the Dead Sea.

Your hair is very straight, but thank goodness, your head is wavy.

Your hair is as wavy as the ocean. And your face looks like something that washed up on the beach.

And your hair is very straight. Not at all like your teeth.

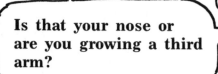

Is that your nose or are you growing a third arm?

Look who's talking. When you try to follow your nose, you have to make two trips.

Is that your nose or did your face put down landing gear?

Look who's talking. If your nose grows any bigger you'll have to wear it in a sling.

Look who's talking. Your nose is so big, it came with training wheels.

Look who's talking. Your nose is so huge, you could sneeze and start World War III.

Look who's talking. Your nose is so big you can smell into the future.

If you were a bank robber, you'd scare more people with your ski mask off.

You wouldn't need a mask if you were a bank robber. You've got the kind of face people try to forget.

You're so ugly the bank asks you to wear a ski mask even when you make a deposit.

You'd have to wear two ski masks. You've got so much ugly, it would leak through one.

You could never be a bank robber. You're too stupid to write the hold-up note.

CHAPTER 6

Use Your Head!

Use your head. It's the little things that count.

Why don't you use *your* head? It doesn't seem to be doing anything.

Use *your* head. I think you'll find it in your back pocket.

You look as if you use your head a lot—as a bowling ball.

Why don't you use your head? It deserves a new experience.

You must use your head a lot. I can see some of the spots where it's starting to get worn.

You could use your head, too. There's a first time for everything.

I'd rather use your head. I prefer one that's never been used.

Do you know how you could lose 12 pounds of ugly fat? Cut your head off.

You don't have to cut *your* head off. It unscrews.

You'd only lose about one pound that way. There's not that much in your head.

You should do the same thing. You'd not only be lighter, but also prettier and smarter.

You know how you could lose 50 pounds of ugly fat? Sit on a Cuisinart.

You know how you could lose 12 pounds of ugly dirt? Wash your socks.

> I think you're very sharp. That's probably because your head comes to a point.

Look who's talking. You could get a job as a stand-in for the Washington Monument.

Look who's talking. As long as you live at home your mother will never have to buy an ice pick.

Look who's talking. Your head is so pointed you're known as the "Human Lightning Rod."

Look who's talking. From the neck up you're built like a hypodermic needle.

Look who's talking about pointy heads. You comb your hair each day with a pencil sharpener.

Your head comes to three points—your nose and both ears.

Look who's talking. Your head's been arrested three times for impersonating a bullet.

Look who's talking about pointy heads. You could wear an ice-cream cone as a hat.

Look who's talking. You're the only person in the world who can put on a dunce cap and have it fit.

You've got a very open mind. That's because of all the holes in your head.

Look who's talking. Your head was the original model for Swiss cheese.

You've got so many holes in your head, on a windy day you whistle.

You've got an open mind, too. It matches your mouth.

You have an open mind, too. That must be how your brain slipped out.

You have a really open mind, too. You're as dumb as all outdoors.

Look who's talking. Your head has almost as many holes as your socks.

You have a closed mind.
It was closed by the
Board of Health.

Thirty years will be just about right. You should be out of secondary school by then.

Yes, come to see me in about thirty years. That'll give me enough time to think of an excuse why I'm not home.

That's about your average, isn't it? You make a new friend about every thirty years or so.

Your teachers have told me it takes you about thirty years to get to know anything.

'Yeah, you can get to know me in about thirty years. But if you really want me to be your friend, you'll make it forty-five.

You know, I'd really like to get to know you better, too. Maybe I'll sign up for biology class.

I'd like to make you my friend, too, but thirty years is awfully short notice.

I'm glad you warned me about that. It gives me a thirty-year head start.

You talk so much—
your tongue has a
racing stripe down
the middle.

You talk so much you're the answer to the question: "What happens when you cross a parrot with a perpetual motion machine?"

You're a person of few words—but not few enough.

You talk so much you carry a spare set of tonsils in your bicycle bag.

You talk so much, you're the only person I ever knew that got a charley horse of the lip.

Your tongue wags so much, two friends have to hold it still long enough for you to brush your teeth.

Look who's talking. You have a black belt in speech.

CHAPTER 7
Go Home!

You've got the kind of face only a mother could love—until she puts on her glasses.

And you're so ugly, when you were born, your mother asked for separate hospitals.

And you're so ugly, every time someone said you looked like your father, it started a fight.

You're so ugly, your baby pictures were printed on an airsick bag.

You've got a face only a mother could love, too. But it did gag the rest of your family.

You're so ugly, you were ten years old before your parents took the bag off your head.

You were so ugly, your parents wanted to trade you back in—for the Elephant Man.

You've got a face only a mother could love, too. Of course, the rest of your body makes her giggle.

Your mother loved your face, too. Because it's what made your father leave town.

Does everybody in your family suffer from insanity?

No, some of them enjoy it.

Your family is so crazy, they added an extra belfry to handle all the bats.

Your family's so goofy, Disney may sue for copyright infringement.

Your family is so weird, at dinnertime they wear shirts, ties, and straitjackets.

Look who's talking. The dodo bird is part of your family crest.

Look who's talking. It's been six generations since anyone in your family has been allowed to play with anything sharp.

Your family is so nutty, when the clock says, "Cuckoo, cuckoo," they all take it personally.

> Your family's favorite poem is:
> Roses are red.
> Violets are blue.
> I'm schizophrenic;
> And so am I.

Your family's so wacky, they don't eat fruit-cake—they worship it as a god.

Look who's talking. In your household bananas is not something to eat—it's a way of life.

Look who's talking. When somebody in your family goes sane, they have him committed.

Why don't you put your nose upside down, take a shower, and drown yourself?

Why don't you jump in a jar of cold cream and soften yourself to death?

Why don't your rub yourself down with peanut butter and stick to the roof of your own mouth?

Why don't you gargle with rocket fuel, burp, and shoot yourself into outer space?

Why don't you suck on a lemon and brighten up your personality?

Why don't you sit on a tack and get a rise out of yourself?

Why don't you rub some tuna fish on your body and go shark hunting?

Your face is a mess. When you get out of bed in the morning from now on, try doing it feet first.

You don't look too good, either. I think you should stop knocking on doors with your nose.

You're not pretty, either. I think carrying suitcases with your teeth has taken its toll.

You're not gorgeous, either. When you slam a door in someone's face from now on, you better make sure it's not your own.

You look beat up, too. Renting out your head as a soccer ball has got to stop.

Is yours a happy family, or do you still live at home?

Your family looks happy enough. I know, I've watched them in the window of the pet store.

Look who's talking about happy family. You were abandoned in a basket on somebody's doorstep—six different times.

You don't know the meaning of the words, "happy family." In fact, there are only about 16 words you do know the meaning of.

I know you still live at home. I saw your mother changing the paper in the bottom of your cage.

I know you still live at home. I can read the address on your pet tag.

CHAPTER 8

You're So Stupid . . .

You're so stupid you think Sherlock Holmes is a row of houses.

And you're so stupid you think Oral Roberts is a mouthwash.

And you're so stupid you think Shirley Temple is a synagogue for children.

And you're so stupid you think Rocky Road is the street that Sylvester Stallone lives on.

And you're so stupid you think the bare necessities is a convenience store in a nudist camp.

And you're so stupid you think Sean Penn is a prison for young actors.

And you're so stupid you think the State Pen is what the Governor uses to write with.

And you're so stupid you think the Kentucky Derby is a hat.

And you're so stupid someone once said, "Look at the dead bird," and you looked up.

Speak up! You're entitled to own your own stupid opinion.

If you ever have a stupid opinion, it would be an improvement.

If I want stupid opinions, I don't speak up; I just listen to you.

I don't need my own stupid opinions. You've got enough of those for everybody.

It's better to be quiet and have people think you're a fool, than speak up, like you, and remove all doubt.

I'd give you my stupid opinion, but you seem to have enough of your own already.

When you're talking there's no need for anyone else's stupid opinions.

Stupid opinions are the only kind your mind can handle.

Have you got a minute?
Tell me everything
you know.

Why don't we take ten seconds and I'll just
tell you the things you'll understand.

If I had a minute, I wouldn't waste it talking
to you.

Why waste our time? I don't think your brain
can hold a minute's worth of information.

Why don't we take half a minute and review
everything you *already* know.

If I did, then you'd be too smart for your
age—which is the Stone Age.

All right. Why don't you turn around and I'll
talk directly to your brain.

That'll be twice as
much time as you've
spent on education up
to now.

You don't always say stupid things—just when your lips are moving.

You should know about lips moving. That's all dummies like you are good for.

I only say stupid things when I'm talking to you. I want to keep the conversation at your level.

The last intelligent things you said were "Ma-ma" and "Da-da."

. . . and that was just last week.

I've been taught to think before I speak. You don't think before, during, or after you speak.

CHAPTER 9

What a Slob!

You know about clean socks, huh? Boy, you have a great memory.

You don't even wear socks. You just paint your ankles with shoe polish.

I like the cologne you're wearing—"Evening at the Bronx Zoo."

I know you don't wear any deodorant. You just hang a Shell "No-Pest Strip" under each arm.

Look who's talking about smell. If you stay in one room too long the police start looking for the dead body.

You should put on clean socks, too—that's if you can scrape the old ones off.

Your body odor is so bad when you go to the beach, the tide goes out and stays there.

Look who's talking. You smell so bad that your own nose tried to file for divorce.

Look who's talking about smell. When you go to the zoo, the monkeys put on gas masks.

Maybe I can borrow some of your cologne— "Janitor in a Drum."

It must be a thrill for you to know someone who wears underwear.

I'm sure you change your underwear often— every time the owner wants it back.

I've heard you change your underwear every day. You change with your brother; your brother changes with your sister . . .

I change my underwear about as often as you clean out your cage.

And I've heard the only time you change
yours is when you find a new pair.

How often do you change your underwear?
Oh, I forgot. You won't know that until you're
potty trained.

You don't even wear underwear. You just have
a "Fruit of the Loom" label tattooed on your
backside.

You change your under-
wear the way trees
change their leaves—
they just change color
and fall off.

Just because you smell like an ape, that doesn't mean you're Tarzan.

Only you would know what an ape smelled like.

When I smell like an ape, I think I'm you.

That's not an ape you smell. It's your breath blowing back in your face.

Apes are the smartest animals next to man, which puts you in third place.

Just because you smell like limburger, that doesn't mean you're the big cheese.

Just because your ears are pointy, that doesn't mean you're Mr. Spock.

Just because you've got a face like a hubcap, that doesn't mean you're a big wheel.

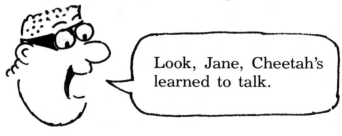

Look, Jane, Cheetah's learned to talk.

You should be an artist. You're good at drawing flies.

You're just the opposite. No decent fly would set foot on you.

If a fly lands on you, the first thing he does is sit down and wash his feet.

The only thing you're good at drawing is criticism.

You could be an artist, too—if they ever let you have anything that's pointy again.

You should be an artist, too. I understand your best subject is still finger painting.

Look who's talking. Your head looks like the bacon grease capital of the world.

Look who's talking. If your hair ever caught fire, it would burn for four days.

Look who's talking. You've got the only head in the world that's been declared a fire hazard.

Have you ever looked at your head? Last week it got six marriage proposals from a greased pig.

And your hair is wild. It looks like your pardon came through 30 seconds after they pulled the switch.

It looks better than yours. Your hair looks like you washed it in a Cuisinart.

I don't think you've combed your hair since the neighbors borrowed your rake.

I've seen hair like yours on scarecrows, but they have the decency to wear a hat.

You don't even go to the barber. You just lay out front when someone mows the lawn.

Your breath is so bad, it's considered chemical warfare.

Look who's talking. You know what they call people who kiss you? Survivors.

Look who's talking. The only thing that would make your breath kissing sweet is fumigation.

Look who's talking. The only good thing about your breath is that it keeps bugs away.

At least I go to the dentist. You get your teeth cleaned by mail.

The last time you went to the dentist, he only found one cavity—your head.

Look who's talking. Your breath is so bad when you enter a room and say "Hi," the wallpaper peels off.

CHAPTER 10

Goodbye and Good Riddance!

You didn't have to say anything. You offend me just by being in the area.

I don't take it personally. Every time you open your mouth, you offend someone.

Well, you probably said it without thinking—the way you do most things.

Don't lose any sleep over it. I haven't listened to anything you've said over the past five years.

Nothing you say could ever offend me. I'm only offended by things that make sense.

I wouldn't be offended by anything you say. I'm just happy that you're stringing words together into sentences now.

It's not what you say; it's the thought behind it that counts. And I know there's never any thought behind anything you say.

I never forget a face, either. I'll remember both of yours.

I may never forget your face either. But I'll spend the rest of my life trying.

It must be easy for you to remember faces. You have absolutely nothing else to clutter your mind.

You'd better commit my face to memory. I'm going to try to make sure you never see it in person again.

It's a shame you never forget faces. I wish you'd forgotten to bring yours today.

You have the memory of an elephant—and the face to go with it.

You're welcome to forget my face if you want. I'm going to try to forget all of you.

Any time I want to remember your face, I can go look at it on the Post Office wall.

Why don't you take a long walk on a short pier?

No, then I'd be all wet—like you.

Why don't you become a small snack for a large snake?

You can't take a long walk. Your leash doesn't go that far.

Why don't you take a short swim *under* a short pier?

Why don't you jump across a well in two jumps?

Why don't you leap a tall building in a single failure?

Why don't you take a long swing from a short rope?

If you took a long walk on a short pier, you'd have to stop and ask directions.

Why don't you hold a long bomb with a short fuse?

Why don't you take a tiny leap into a Grand Canyon?

Why don't you give your big mouth a small vacation?

Why don't you go home and tell your mother she wants you?

Why don't you do the same—or isn't the zoo open yet?

Why don't you tell your father he wants you—or do you have to wait for visiting hours?

Why don't you go home and tell your keeper it's feeding time?

At least I have a home to go to. You just slide under a rock.

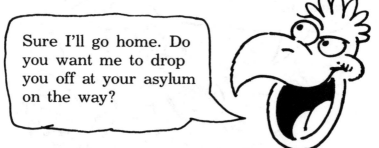

Sure I'll go home. Do you want me to drop you off at your asylum on the way?

About the Author

Gene Perret was born in Philadelphia, Pennsylvania. He began his career in comedy while he was working at General Electric, emceeing company banquets and parties. In 1969 his hobby became a full-time profession when he left GE to write for Bob Hope, Phyllis Diller, Carol Burnett, Bill Cosby, Tim Conway, and many other stars.

A few of the TV shows he has written for are: *Laugh-In*, *The Jim Nabors Hour*, *The Carol Burnett Show*, and *The Bill Cosby Show*. He produced and wrote *Welcome Back, Kotter*, *Three's Company*, and the *Tim Conway Show*.

Gene is now Bob Hope's head writer. He travels all over the world, working on Bob Hope's television specials and personal appearances. And, in his spare time, Gene performs his own brand of after-dinner humor for associations and corporations all across the country.

He has earned three Emmy awards for his writing and one Writer's Guild award.

Gene lives in San Marino, California, with his wife, Joanne. His four children, Joe, Terry, Carole, and Linda, are grown and on their own, so he's now beginning to write material for grandsons Michael and Brett.

Index